THE PORTAGE POETRY SERIES

SERIES TITLES

Time Traveling
Kate Deimling

The Worse for Wear
Jenna Goldsmith

Mouth
Amorak Huey

Little Joy
Matthew Murrey

When I Was Baptized in Missouri Dirt
Chad Parmenter

The Vinegar in Our Hearts: Triolets
Jesse DeLong

The Weather of Our Names
Cal Freeman

Temporary Shelters
Grant Clauser

Pandora's Prairie
Katherine Hoerth

An Introduction to Error
Deirdre Lockwood

tic tic tic
Heidi Seaborn

And the Heart Will Not Quicken
Russell Thorburn

Wildfire
Corie Rosen

Lost Cathedral
Hannah Rodabaugh

Exile Is Home
Elvis Alves

Even the Sky
Kevin Thomason

How We Argue
Sharon Kouros

The Underdream
Aiyana Masla

Dining on Salt: Four Seasons of Septets
Wayne Lee

Torrential
Jayne Marek

Users with Access: New and Selected Poems
Brandon Krieg

Flu Season
Katie Kalisz

No Trouble Staying Awake
Teresa Scollon

Another Native Tongue
Susan Riley Clarke

Catch & Release
Lauren Crawford

Steelhead
Lauren K. Carlson

The Coronation of the Ghost
Benjamin Gantcher

The Stone Tries to Understand the Hands
Susannah Sheffer

Red Camaro
Dwaine Rieves

Where Babies Come From
Ori Fienberg

Cuttings
Hannah Dow

Forgive the Animal
Sarah Pape

Love as Invasive Species
Ellen Kombiyil

They Were Horrible Cooks
Allison Whittenberg

The New Life
Wendy Wisner

Restoring Prairie
Margaret Rozga

Table with Burning Candle
Julia Paul

A Bright Wound
Sarah A. Etlinger

The Velvet Book
Rae Gouirand

Listening to Mars
Sally Ashton

Glitter City
Bonnie Jill Emanuel

The Trouble with Being a Childless Only Child
Michelle Meyer

Happy Everything
Caitlin Cowan

Dear Lo
Brady Bove

Sadness of the Apex Predator
Dion O'Reilly

Do Not Feed the Animal
Hikari Miya

The Watching Sky
Judy Brackett Crowe

Let It Be Told in a Single Breath
Russell Thorburn

The Blue Divide
Linda Nemec Foster

Lake, River, Mountain
Mark B. Hamilton

Talking Diamonds
Linda Nemec Foster

Poetic People Power
Tara Bracco (ed.)

The Green Vault Heist
David Salner

There is a Corner of Someplace Else
Camden Michael Jones

Everything Waits
Jonathan Graham

We Are Reckless
Christy Prahl

Always a Body
Molly Fuller

Bowed As If Laden With Snow
Megan Wildhood

Silent Letter
Gail Hanlon

New Wilderness
Jenifer DeBellis

Fulgurite
Catherine Kyle

The Body Is Burden and Delight
Sharon White

Bone Country
Linda Nemec Foster

Not Just the Fire
R.B. Simon

Monarch
Heather Bourbeau

The Walk to Cefalù
Lynne Viti

The Found Object Imagines a Life: New and Selected Poems
Mary Catherine Harper

Naming the Ghost
Emily Hockaday

Mourning
Dokubo Melford Goodhead

Messengers of the Gods: New and Selected Poems
Kathryn Gahl

After the 8-Ball
Colleen Alles

Careful Cartography
Devon Bohm

Broken On the Wheel
Barbara Costas-Biggs

Sparks and Disperses
Cathleen Cohen

Holding My Selves Together: New and Selected Poems
Margaret Rozga

Lost and Found Departments
Heather Dubrow

Marginal Notes
Alfonso Brezmes

The Almost-Children
Cassondra Windwalker

Meditations of a Beast
Kristine Ong Muslim

Time Traveling

As her title implies, Kate Deimling offers us meditations formal and informal on the vicissitudes of time. More specifically, how best to manage its ravages and double-crossings. Hint: it helps if you don't sit still in one time zone. Enter Lot's wife. Enter a figure skater after she crashes. Enter the three-legged dog that romps with the best, and the Roman emperor who would rather grow cabbages than rule Rome again. The collection opens and opens, leaving room for Deimling's own stories and ours. And what do you do when a friend jumps from a dorm window but only breaks his leg? You take scones to the hospital and talk about the big snow.

—LANCE LARSEN
author of *Making a Kingdom of It*
former Poet Laureate of Utah

Time travel can be a way to think of human time in relation to the more-than-human, the natural world that surrounds our human habitations. And Deimling's evocation of other literary works leads us to the imaginative time travel we find in books, especially as writers learning from those who came before, reaching out to those who will read us after we're gone. Deimling explores all these aspects of time in a thoughtful collection that rewards a reader's attention.

—SUSANNA LANG
author of *Like This*

These poems hone our sense of life's elapsing. This book is an arm around our shoulders—solace and encouragement on our brief and endless travels through the present.

—JED MYERS
author of *Learning to Hold*

In this taut debut collection of poetry laced with the formalism of sonnets and ghazals, Kate Deimling's translator-trained ear is in evidence in the rhythms and rhymes infusing her words. These poems sing as we're urged to "find meaning where we may."

—NANCY NAOMI CARLSON
author of *Piano in the Dark*
winner of the Oxford-Weidenfeld Translation Prize

Time Traveling

poems

Kate Deimling

CORNERSTONE PRESS
UNIVERSITY OF WISCONSIN-STEVENS POINT

Cornerstone Press, Stevens Point, Wisconsin 54481
Copyright © 2026 Kate Deimling
www.uwsp.edu/cornerstone

Printed in the United States of America.

Library of Congress Control Number: 2026931104
ISBN: 978-1-968148-30-0

Cover art © Marcel.la Barceló. Courtesy of the artist and HdM Gallery.

Cornerstone Press titles are produced in courses and internships offered by the
Department of English at the University of Wisconsin–Stevens Point.

DIRECTOR & PUBLISHER
Dr. Ross K. Tangedal

EXECUTIVE EDITORS
Jeff Snowbarger, Freesia McKee

EDITORIAL DIRECTOR
Brett Hill

SENIOR EDITORS
Paige Biever, Reilly Crous

PRESS STAFF
Allison Lange, Eleanor Belcher, John Evans, Sophie McPherson, Sam Bjork,
Madison Schultz, Autumn Vine

For Brian, Clara, and Julian

CONTENTS

I

When Someone Says *I've Never Looked Back* 3
To My Daughter on Her Eighteenth Birthday 4
3:45 PM 6
Counting the Miles 8
By the Clock 9
Fall 10
The Other Pool 11
Spaying the Dog 13
All the Linden Trees in Bloom 15
Norwegian Wood 16

II

Magnolia Warbler in Central Park 21
Jamaica Bay Wildlife Refuge 22
On Buying a Piece of Water Buffalo Horn as a Chew Toy
for My Dog 23
Kudzu 24
On the Wing 25
Villanelle with Tulips 26
Adaptive Evolution 27
Whales 28
Hiking to the Waterfall 29

III

Evel Knievel in the Café 33
From His Coy Mistress 34
On the Ocean Liner 36
Diocletian's Villanelle 37

Duel 38

Lascaux 41

To Emily Dickinson 42

The Six Swans 43

IV

My Heart 47

Satisfaction 48

Warning 49

Near Ghazal for William Shatner 50

Insomnia 51

Turning Off the Blood 52

After the Opera 54

Pinned 56

The Camperdown Elm, Prospect Park 58

Barn Owl 59

V

TFW 63

Where Are the Snows of Yesteryear? 64

The Three-Legged Dog at the Dog Park 65

To the Figure Skater Who Fell 66

Why I'm Making Scones 68

Ghazal for God 70

The Book of the Dead 71

Scene with Dog 72

Thin Times 74

Waiting for the Subway 75

Acknowledgments 77

I.

When Someone Says *I've Never Looked Back*

I don't believe them. I've looked many times,
just to measure what might have been. I've let
my life unravel like a piece of twine
and traced other strands to imagined ends.
At times I'm frightened when I think how much
things could have been changed, with an offer turned
down, a letter astray, an egg untouched,
securely closed to aimless, drifting sperm.
I guess I want to be assured. Rewind
and still reject the B side's unplayed track.
Like Lot's wife as she checks that all behind
her burns. She stands nameless on the vacant
plain, hardened to salt. I would have glanced back
myself, just to glimpse the road not taken.

To My Daughter on Her Eighteenth Birthday

Radiant woman
once in my womb,
you pose for a photo

on this bright morning
of bare-limbed trees
and I feel you've burst forth

fully formed,
eyes clear as Athena's.
Eighteen years speed

by as in a dream
of hard-won sleep
after a glass of dark beer

to bring down my milk
with the Moses basket wedged
next to me on the bed

as the cat peers over the edge,
withdrawing a paw
in surprise.

Time telescopes once more—
my back is bent
and you present me

with a daughter of your own,
the crook of my arm nestling
her head with its bones still closing

and I look into her eyes
as they start to seek the shapes
of faces, soon ready to gaze

back. Will my emotions
deepen again, intense
as honey's crystal grit?

Now my hand cradles
these first pictures of you
as an adult, and I recall

the long December night
of my lived miracle,
the doctor cutting through seven layers

and peeling back my muscle
to gather you up,
turning the tight ball of you

to face me over the curtain
and handing you to my husband in scrubs
as I waited my turn

to hold you before you learned to walk,
with that firm purpose
of yours, away from me.

3:45 PM

I walk around the house synchronizing
clocks that have crept ahead or dropped

behind. When did these floorboards edge apart?
The house has shifted, not an even

angle to be found. The chairs are all tucked snug
around the dining table, which bears

only a pair of candles. The windows have clouded over
like old eyes. Outside,

a few shoots have poked through soil
as a blue jay chirps, replacing its raucous call.

Once the hour of coming home, stacking cookies
on a plate, their centers seeded with fruit,

this time now lies inert, like the dog
curled on her cushion.

I grab the green fan of crooked carrots wrinkled with dirt.
I feel the bumps and valleys of fist-sized potatoes,

probe their scars with the point of the knife,
cut and pile them in the baking dish

burned brown in the corners, though it's too much
for one. I picture how the potatoes' flesh

will soften, their skin sliding loose.
The porcelain sink is marked

with cracks that thread their way like rivers
mapping a foreign land.

I've already cleared all the cobwebs, sent the spiders
outside for better hunting.

The face of the stainless steel fridge
shines, sheer as a rock monument.

Counting the Miles

Leaving the hospital, we carefully thread
the belt through the car seat slots
with our son's small, cushioned head
looking backward to the rear-view void.

Since he sees at most a few feet,
it doesn't much matter which way he's aimed.
Yet it's troubling up here in the front seat
to see in the mirror just a plastic shell.

Soft, bright blankets drape his fresh skin,
and, as the engine comes to life, our new car
measures miles in the single digits as we begin
the trip home, merging into the flow. As we cross

the bridge, glancing at the pointed waves below,
the metal grid rattles and slides under our wheels.
How many miles will we cover, watching him grow—
when this number climbs to a hundred thousand

or more, will the rusted frame of this van
deliver him to some new home, his head
almost brushing the ceiling, a man
moving into a future we hardly conceive?

By the Clock

Fall Back

The day is only one hour longer
but time loosens its stitches
like a hem undone
so a child's pants instantly grow.
Darkness drops like a curtain at show's end.

Spring Forward

The day is only one hour shorter
but leaps ahead on insect legs.
Then night sneaks in,
the moon hanging low, shamefaced
to show up so late.

Fall

Overnight it's grown too cool
to keep windows open.
I awake chilled
to vacant sky, the sun
out of sight.

I'm unprepared.
I need to wear something warm,
but it's all packed away.
I find long sleeves, tall socks,
stick my sandals in the closet.

Already this descent
into winter, already wind alone
at play on the beaches
where waves spike,
sand hard as tundra.

In the yard, the geraniums
are sparse, with leaves that curl
at the edge. Dried blossoms
I haven't removed
stand shriveled and dark.

Eleven years since fall
and death came swiftly on,
my father in his tomb,
sky pressing clouds
upon the stones.

Is this how Persephone felt?
Still flushed with summer's warm
forgetting, called back to the underworld,
creeping down a black cavern,
every moment a farewell?

The Other Pool

The main pool in town was enormous,
Olympic. The right side swarmed with kids,
bodies bobbing, splashing, dunking
to the screech of the lifeguard's whistle.

The left side stirred with the clockwork
rotation of serious swimmers, lithe bodies
enlaced by water, their swim-capped heads
like Chinese checkers advancing for the win.

My mother and I went to the other pool:
neglected, near the seedy side of town,
with yellowed windows where light had the hue
of my Polaroid baby pics.

Old neighborhood ladies plodded
through the water, mouths surfacing
to open like sedate frogs. I'd watch
their broad bodies struggle up the ladder

and stand there dripping, jaws clenching
and opening, like displaced fish. I swam laps
alongside my mom, then played a game
where she held and suddenly dropped me.

She could only lift me because of my buoyancy
in water—I was getting much too big,
but it felt natural to be supported by her arms.
Cradled, I'd kick my legs and wait

to descend to that silent kingdom
for a moment of floating free
before my feet found the bottom
and I stood to do it again. It didn't bother us—

or anyone—to be the only ones at play.
Coming and going, the old women
nodded, waved their fingers hello, goodbye,
mentioned grandbabies, or disease.

Leaving, they loosened the chin straps
on their swim caps, while the lifeguard let
one flip-flop dangle, ankles crossed.
What beauty there was to it all—

the women plowing through the water,
beams of light carving the air,
waves lapping at the edge as I was launched
in the last game of my childhood.

Spaying the Dog

I

The dog comes home with a white cone
called an *Elizabethan collar*
but more like a dunce cap.
She hangs her head and won't stir.

We scoot her along the floor,
but she will not stand, and she weighs
nearly one hundred pounds. We buy
an inflatable ring to replace

the cone, and now she relaxes,
flops on the floor. I see the valley
carved by the wound in her skin,
six inches cut vertically,

like C-section scars in the old days.
Mine is horizontal, lower.
Loose skin smiles above it when
I'm naked in front of the mirror.

On the floor, back toes pointing
like a ballerina's, she stretches
to her full length, lets out a snort.
The dog isn't self-conscious.

No exercise for fourteen days.
It's done, and she's safe. Yet
knowing she'll never swell with life
I feel a shadow of regret.

II

Stitches dissolved and wound healed,
the dog goes out to play.
When she grows old, I suppose
joy will no longer raise

her front paws from the floor
when told *backyard* or *park*. She pulls
on the leash, legs electric,
but one day they'll stiffen, hobble

across the kitchen tile, nails
clicking. The arc of dogs' lives
is contained within the curve of ours.
Already her genes won't survive.

Heel, slow down. We work on commands
as we walk. Now my daughter bends
to unhook the leash, grasps the collar
tight, lets the dog through the fence

and she bounds off, paws pounding.
She touches muzzles here, darts
there, bows low, her tail swaying high.
Then she comes back to where we are,

leans against our legs, and I feel
we three are one, on this cloudless
afternoon, as shafts of sun
light the new green leaves above us.

All the Linden Trees in Bloom

The last day of school is done,
backpack light as air, and I'm zipping
down the street on my bike.
A boy from my class waves

by the fence—he likes me,
I think, and I smile and keep on riding.
I swerve around a pothole and glide
on freshly laid pavement, smooth

as frosting. My pocket holds
money for a snowball and I can already
see the syrup pouring down, drenching
the icy surface in orange or red.

The hydrangea bursts
with purple globes and there's that freaky
ginkgo tree, older than the dinosaurs.
The tip of my ponytail tickles

my neck, and all my muscles
feel taut. *Summer*—the word
wets my mouth with the tang
of sour candy, bounces

around my brain like the announcement
of a miracle. I curve around the corner
in perfect control, I'm twelve years old
and I can do anything

with no thought for time,
the pure hot air firing
my blood, as a sweet scent drifts down
from all the linden trees in bloom.

Norwegian Wood

Elongated faces of boys with bowl cuts
circled the record cover
whose groovy script oozed mystery
to the ten-year-old girl I was.

A petroleum fossil
of my mother's former life,
the record was etched with history—
a time when John Lennon was alive

and my mother was single
and known to smoke a cigarette
as I'd seen in old photos, her mod
haircut framing a different smile.

But the voices chimed and poured
into the present. Why didn't my mother stir
from the armchair where she graded papers?
The music moved me—it rose and fell

clanging in anger, then gently pleading.
I sang the lyrics like sacred verse,
floored by the second song:
he didn't have the girl,

the girl had *him*.
Would I ever possess
a person like that? My parents
sat silently in separate rooms

as I swayed, arms loose, to the music,
hair uncombed, wearing a t-shirt
with peeling decals. I didn't think
Norwegian wood was furniture. I pictured

a forest looming at the song's edge waiting
to be explored. Hearing this song again—
tinny this time, hand-held—I can't say
I'm transported to that wood-paneled den.

So much time has passed
since then. But those opening chords,
sharp and yearning, still pluck
at something I'm not sure I understand.

II.

Magnolia Warbler in Central Park

Kinetic, frenetic,
flitting, falling,
a tiny tang of light.

Its body trills
up and down tips of trees.
Find it, and it's gone—

no, settled for a second.
Black and white dapple
its top like spots of shade.

Now the taut belly turns
to us, flashy as a taxi
with jaunty black bands.

Imagine inside
a pea-sized heart
that taps and taps away,

the empty bones
always lifting, lifting,
as the bird is borne

into the light, rises,
itself a drop of light,
a bright particle

interrupting the air.

Jamaica Bay Wildlife Refuge

We're in a tunnel of leaves
bristling the air as swallows dip and glide
and we can already smell the sea.

Vines dangle their rosy trumpets
and the yucca points a tower of petals
toward the sky. Our feet grind the gravel

and I wish I could move low and sleek
like the rabbits who join the pines,
haunches vanishing like shadows.

When the bushes fall away
the bay opens wide to pull in
tongues of sand where the wind

fluffs the reeds. Water surrounds us
on this strip between salt and fresh,
the bay sliding to the shore,

the pond barred with light.
Sandpipers scissor their legs, speeding
across the mudflats to spear for bugs.

When an egret flicks its wings
and stills, we follow its gaze
into the distance we've come here for.

A jet angles into the sky as the sun sculpts
the edges all around us and I wonder—
how can anyone be leaving now?

On Buying a Piece of Water Buffalo Horn as a Chew Toy for My Dog

Amidst the bins of crisp cod and marrow bones
there's a polished mahogany cylinder
smooth in my hand. The tag gives no origin,
just says *water buffalo horn*, and I imagine

this animal standing by the Ganges, tips
of fur stirred in the wind, mouth
sinking to munch on patches of grass,
broad, dark eyes reflecting the sky.

I tell myself there can be no profit
in selling only the horn, right?
They slaughter the beast for meat,
send its horn to the States

through this vast web
of economy uniting us all
so my dog can sit and stare
with the same focus she applies

to a stick, open her muzzle
with its quivering whiskers,
and clamp down on the remnant
of this ruminant's showy finery

from eight thousand miles away
in this dog-eat-water-buffalo world.

Kudzu

It roves free and greedy,
creeps speedily
up the trees,
transforms telephone poles
with a heavy sheath of leaves.

To spread its breed,
the mad vine embraces branches,
fondles foliage,
gropes the ground
in a sheet of green.

It seeks to assimilate all,
cleaves through unbelievers,
seethes with conviction
that vegetation must convert
to its creed.

Like a single teeming being
it flutters for miles in the breeze.
Its unchecked course continues,
invader of landscapes,
draper of evil Eden.

On the Wing

The green-winged teal
is mostly drab, the color of cloudy
mushroom soup or military
fatigues that blend
into desert sand.

But catch it in flight,
wings spread wide, and see those feathers
fan out white, then fade to dark again
at the tips, like a trick
of the light.

There on the wing's surface,
edged with black, is a green
panel, in the very spot I've gazed at
from seat 22A—the flap on an airplane
wing that tilts up

during takeoff, increasing lift.
Does this bright device
of feathers adjust air flow
as the duck steers through routes
mapped by instinct, over wind-fanned fields

and trickling rivers stilled by distance?
Tracing invisible lines through air, tethered
between cloud and earth, can the bird
feel its part in this perfect geometry
as I spy that square of green vanishing in the sky?

Villanelle with Tulips

They come back like magic,
pushing up through the ground
overnight, a burst of music.

Soon leaves will part, unfold like fabric;
tomorrow, petals tightly bound,
they come back like magic.

You don't get this show in the tropics.
Winter's drab, but spring puts on her gown
overnight, a burst of music

for pollen transport—a flashy gimmick
for bees and butterflies that flit around
(they come back like magic).

We're put to shame by plant logistics.
They've got their timing down:
overnight, a burst of music.

Tulip, crocus, dogwood—with a flick
of a switch, spring turns on the sound:
they come back like magic,
overnight, a burst of music.

Adaptive Evolution

Tell me this isn't a miracle: weeks go by
as infant tortoises dig inch by inch
through dark soil to feel the light.
An eye migrates over the flat head of a fish
as it scoots along the sand. Pelagic
birds might not touch land for a year, but soar
to nesting grounds where they once hatched as chicks
in the same slot in the cliff years before.
Leave it to humans to make this a mess.
DDT weakened eggshells so they split;
oil spills matted feathers, froze birds to death.
But we're changing too, right? We can't predict
how we might be reborn, what we might claw
our way out of, as we trade dirt for dawn.

Whales

Mammals like us,
they transformed with tails
into creatures of the sea,
with bellies tough as hulls
and huge heads for prows.

Forearms flattened
and spread into fins,
legs retracted
into traces of bones
still found in their flanks.

The oil-filled foreheads
echo with mysterious songs:
the beluga's canary chirps,
the humpback's oboe moans.
We wonder what it means.

We chant our promised land,
the sea, intone the tales
of the measureless deep
where we roam, cradled
by the watery womb of the world.

Hiking to the Waterfall

From a distance, it's like the roar
of cars, a highway traffic hum.
But let's say we hear water pour
and gurgle, since the reason we've come

is to escape all those city sounds
and *get back in touch with nature,*
break our routine. Uneven ground
dips, and, with long legs, my partner

strides ahead, as I study where
to step between roots on the trail
slick with pine needle layers.
Rectangular markers are nailed

to the trees. My eyes scan for them,
like finding icons on my laptop.
Hike as task—just one more item
to be checked off the list. It never stops,

this need to always be doing
something. I yank on the strap, adjust
the weight of my pack. Protruding
ferns bend underfoot as we rush

downward. My heels begin to burn
with each smack on the dirt. Sunblock
stings my left eye. We turn
past a screen of leaves and spot

falling water in a bright crash
feeding the pool, skirting the stones.
The outspread wings of a hawk slash
the sky arched above this shadowed

gathering of trees where our breath
blows ragged. I think we both feel
this sense something's been left
behind, shrugged off, as our skin sealed

with sweat meets the mist. Soon we'll talk
but for now we take it in, see
flecks of light flash upon worn rocks
washed over by the rushing stream.

III.

Evel Knievel in the Café

Even the streetlamps are tired, and blink
like weak stars. Melted wax is stuck
to the tablecloth like a seal. Only in a drink
does an olive taste good, when you can suck
the liquor from it. Lettuce like a fan on my plate.
She praises the silver of my hair.
"You still have your pick of the girls," my pal said late
last night, poking an elbow into the air
safely near my ribs. But the nerves can't jar
themselves. Only when your body makes a fault
in space, while flowers near the track
shake and grope for air. The blurred cars
rise to trip up your wheel, sun softens the asphalt,
and the sky like a mouth hangs slack.

From His Coy Mistress

After Andrew Marvell (1621–1678)

I hesitate to lift my pen
and answer you, most wise of men,
who by your phrases stretch all time
so I can see a mountain climb
from cracks beneath and rainy haze
begin a Flood which mounts with praise
you heap upon each eye, each breast,
allowing eons to the rest!
Like Aphrodite I could reign;
while worlds decline your love would gain.
But she would love you straightaway;
gods have no rules they must obey,
no mothers guarding pride and purse,
no fathers willing fast to curse
a foolish girl swayed by your lines.
But now what words from one who pines!
Soon time contracts; before I hear
how charming and lovely and dear
I am, you've tossed me in the grave!
A new technique indeed—to rave
that worms chew up my flesh. Perhaps
our brilliant pens, like modern maps,
have charted all the pretty climes
and left the bogs for gruesome rhymes.
But I am very much alive—
why, yesterday alone saw five
young men who vied to serve my tea;
they surely would not bend their knee
before a corpse. It's rather queer
for me to picture death so near.
The rest of life appears so long;
I have not heard the swan's slow song
and all my life I have been young.
Apologies if you've been stung,

but if I'm coy, it earns me time
and slows the sun whose endless climb
you fear so much. I fear it too
but won't devour a fruit whose new
skin soon will rot; I'd rather move
to find a wine time will improve.
I can't forbid the sun to burn
our days in fire, but I can turn
those iron gates to gates of gold
and grasp the heavens in my hold.

On the Ocean Liner

The sun, that injured hound, began to slink into its hole.
The passengers lined the deck like ducks.
They held their hats, swallowed their tea, became
uneasy. The young woman gripped a hairpin in her mouth
with the grimace of a gunfighter.
Her blond hair emerged
from her black part, visible as sin.
There! No more would her locks
hover near her face like an anxious waiter
in this impossible wind.

The waves grabbed the railing
like drowning men. Wet, unmanageable,
the deck was a dare.
By gum, I'll make it to the aft doors,
the young man muttered to himself.
His sole skated through a puddle,
lost purchase, and he fell
flat on his back. Someone stood above him,
arms akimbo, outlined in the dying light,
hair blown into two golden wings.

"Hello, angel," he said, and laughed.
Her hand approached as if from the sky.

Diocletian's Villanelle

Diocletian was the only Roman emperor
to retire voluntarily. When two officials
came to try to persuade him to return to
Rome and resume control, he told them he
preferred growing cabbages.

You should see these cabbages of mine
fan their generous green leaves…and their size—
massive, stretching in an endless line.

I'm aware an emperor is divine,
and it's kind of you to call me wise—
you should see these cabbages of mine.

Oh, yes, how the city did shine,
her marble monuments reaching to the skies,
massive, stretching in an endless line,

but here, since I have resigned,
I have secured a valuable prize:
you should see these cabbages of mine,

as plentiful as grapes on the vine,
as big around as one of your thighs—
massive, stretching in an endless line.

I'm afraid I must respectfully decline
to return as emperor, but please, come, rise,
you should see these cabbages of mine,
massive, stretching in an endless line.

Duel

The Journalist

The sun pierced his eyes.
It was still warm
and he felt almost happy
in this little clearing—
what a nice spot for a picnic with Florine!
He laughed inside at his foolishness
and felt his hand tremble on the door handle.
His friend handed him a flask
and he took a swig.
Dead leaves lay at his feet
like a pile of rumpled clothes.
He grasped the knot of his tie
and remembered her straightening it
this morning, laughing,
kissing him for luck
as he left for what he told her
was an interview.
Why write that stupid article? Why stoop
so low? It was too late now.
Anyway, it's true enough,
he thought, handing off his jacket.
He caught himself
counting the paces to the center.
He listened to the instructions and walked away.
One — two — three —
four — five — six —
seven — eight — nine —
ten — spin and fire.
He heard the blast, smelled the sting
of sulfur and metal, and saw
smoke waft away
as from an extinguished candle
and the other man stagger

backward like that bad actor
who was met with howls of laughter
when he held his side
and tumbled to the ground,
legs absurdly askew.

The Aristocrat

Sunlight was glinting
through the stunned trees
as he stepped out, his polished shoes
slowly folding the grass.
He tried to slam the door
with conviction. In the clearing,
the wind stung his face like an insult.
Removing his jacket
as he did last week for his tailor,
he thought, will my new suit
be ready for Amélie's ball on the ninth?
I hope I made it sufficiently clear.
Any delay would be unacceptable.
A waiting arm received the jacket.
A hand clapped his shoulder.
They were striding to meet the others.
Dry leaves crumpled like newspaper
under his feet. He swelled his chest
to accommodate the beating of his heart.
A smear on his name could not be endured,
he reminded himself. This hack, this fool,
was he as careless with a pistol as with a pen?
Pauses all around, then rules read,
and they were pacing off.
One — two — three —
four — five — six —
seven — eight — nine —
Amélie's ball — ten.
Like a dancer, he turned fast.

The air thundered,
his ribs burned,
and the ground pressed against his back
like a chair pushed in for a lady at table.
The linen sky shone
and he struggled to keep his eyes open
as he did when a child, wanting desperately
to descend for the grown-ups' party,
late, so late, into the night.

Lascaux

All is shadow until
light flickers or flashes
and stone walls quicken
with a galloping procession:

cantering antelope,
horse with sun-soaked flank,
spotted bull that gives its twin
a look of recognition.

A bristly-maned horse is dwarfed
by a massive bull, head bowed.
In the corridors of the cave,
one room is called *apse*, another *nave*,

linking this house of creatures
assembled by a brush
and spun into stories
whose sounds spanned the air

with skyward thrusting stone
harboring in glowing glass a man
holding a lamb, while hovers
above him a dove.

To Emily Dickinson

Words thrash,
worms in the wet.

You riddle my wits,
pin Eternity's wings

to a board. You fix
the taut line –

the horizon –
score the Wood

and I am there
where you crease blades

of grass abuzz with Bees
and mark the petal's fall.

What is Felt – is Thought –
is Felt once more –

and to Inhabit your pulse
is – this moment – to believe

we – like bulbs – snug, insensate
below frozen ground –

will Rise
come some Spring!

The Six Swans

Transformed, my brothers flapped frightfully,
twisting their necks, taking off into empty sky.
I had to be silent for six years to save them
and sew six shirts of aster flowers

but the last was unfinished, and so
in place of his left arm, my youngest brother
has a wing. When my skin throbs
with heat he fans me, sweeping it back and forth.

Sometimes I weep to feel these feathers
and their minor power—for what good
is one wing? I wonder at those tender bones
I cannot see, the prickly flesh

never touched by sun, the vanished fingers
and what they might grasp.
But he holds me close, that white span
folded over my back, and whispers

If we are men at all, it's because of you.

IV.

My Heart

My heart is a circus
whose entrance is emblazoned with bulbs,
bright or burned out.
Every clown is oddly familiar.
The shooting gallery and the coin toss
may be rigged. The lion tamer,
whose moustache resembles my father's,
makes the beasts rise up and dance.
The elephants, their hide
like dusty leather-bound books,
link trunks and tails through habit
or resignation. Under the big top,
I put on a death-defying act,
leaping from the trapeze without a net.
The bored populace prefers
the garish display of the freak show
where a man hammers a nail through his tongue
and Zenobia caresses serpents with a look
that could pass for love.
The two-headed baby in the jar
stares at me like a punishment.
In the wee hours,
everything empties out,
the stunned animals sleep,
the new moon is shrouded with clouds.

Satisfaction

About desire they were never wrong,
the Rolling Stones: how well they understood
not getting what you want, young
though you were, and your cloud
occupied. Everyday grief
knows no shelter, the pain of wanting
shines sharp as a blade. But each
year that passes keeps blunting
the tip that touches your flesh.
When's the last time you will bleed?
The old champagne goes flat
and you've shed your crumpled dress.
You know you get what you need.
Can you be satisfied with that?

Warning

The heat may be slow.
The loud music, unpleasant.
Sometimes there's not much to eat.
Look out for anything
unusual. The routine
may appear dull
at first. Buses
are often late.
Playing cards, like many things,
is a waste of time.
Money is hard to come by.
You'll have to get used
to being alone. Others
will demand your time.
Nights are long. Try
singing, or tell yourself stories.
Later you'll wonder
where did all the time go?
The landscape isn't much.
You may become bored. Remember
to seek help. Advice
isn't very reliable.
Sometimes it's hard
to fall asleep
or get up in the morning.
There is no magic solution.
There is no secret signal.
There is no use delaying.

Near Ghazal for William Shatner

"There was no mystery, no majestic awe to behold; all I
saw was death. I saw a cold, dark, black emptiness....
Everything I had thought was wrong. Everything I
had expected to see was wrong."
   —William Shatner on traveling to outer space at age 90

Do not go boldly across that final frontier.
Squeezed in your old Starfleet duds, you'll find it's not a frontier

at all, just cold, unforgiving nowhere, and gazing
on the blue planet, you feel desperate, undone. Fear

rubberizes your guts, and though you didn't hope for green women
with bouffant hairdos who slide their hands across your chest, it was unclear

that space would sap your senses so, leaving you
adrift, with no freedom, no exhilaration—none! Mere

survival's at stake behind a flimsy metal membrane to keep
the void at bay. There's no earth or sun near

your body, they're objects floating behind glass, blinking like nightlights
in darkness that boggles your mind. Fun, cheer,

hope—a lost language your lips can no longer sound. Home beckons
even as it loosens from memory's grip. You'd banked on freer

horizons, but found yourself truly alone, William. Yet you learned
from this trip: you know beauty's not sown in the stars, it's with us, down here.

Insomnia

At night my eyelids flutter like birds—
crazy ones, like in Hitchcock.
Thought upon thought
upon thought lines up in my head
like ducks to be shot at the fair.
Melting ice caps—my friend
who hasn't called—did I pay
the Visa bill? My poor brain
is the carrion the vultures of worry
swoop down on and cover
with their big black wings.
The ant-pile hours accumulate.
I see the digital numbers change
like a pattern of red-hot pokers
rearranged. In my febrile movements
I feel the agony of a dying insect
and the uselessness. Trapped
on the flypaper sheet,
I stare outside at motionless leaves,
extinguished windows,
the dumb pale moon,
and wish I could wake up the world.

Turning Off the Blood

Taken from parental reviews of the video game
Assassin's Creed IV: Black Flag

Look, we're a strictly PG family.
Somehow this game got the rating *mature*—
this doesn't make sense. You play a pirate
seeking his fortune. There's some violence, sure,

and the pirate's not a great role model
but he's not exactly bad. You must stop
people from taking over the city.
The violence is not over the top.

My son's about to turn thirteen—
I said no to Grand Theft Auto and Call
of Duty, but this game's different I think.
No body parts or limbs come off at all.

There's an f-word twice but he's heard that
before. In the tavern you can knock back
shots of rum, but after five you are drunk,
and if you drink even more, you will black

out and wake up in a haystack. There is
cannon fire, a strangling animation,
sword fights during battles on the ship, but
absolutely NO decapitation.

As a protective middle-aged Christian
mom, what is best about this game I found
is that you can turn off the blood. The bad
language in that case will also go down.

Another thing I should mention
is that if innocent people get harmed
you'll be punished. Consequences happen,
so I see no reason to be alarmed

if your son wants to play this game. Violence
in real life should be nipped in the bud,
but in a game, it's not such a big deal—
just don't forget you can turn off the blood.

After the Opera

When the curtain closed, blazing light burst
apart the dark. My hands still stinging
from applause, I groped for my purse
on the floor, as everyone stood, seat bottoms

flipping upright, and turned on my phone
which lit up with a photo of my son's face,
blood blooming next to his eye, a purplish tone
underneath, with a text from his friend's mom

about the accident: he was pulling on a strap
for strength training and the metal clip
attaching it to the doorknob suddenly snapped
and flew at his face. They stopped the bleeding,

but he might need stitches, and could we decide
what we want to do and give them a call?
We made our way down the velvet stairs and outside
into the cold night air. From the photo,

his doctor thought there was risk of a scar,
and ideal timing for stitches on the face
is within twelve hours, so we went to the ER.
It was close to midnight, and we waited

in the exam room interminably,
with an endless loop of ice cream shakes
and hamburgers and detergent pods on TV,
until an intern in teal scrubs bustled in,

cleaned the wound, drew out a long, scary
needle to numb the area, and sewed the gash
with three deep stitches. All quite ordinary
for her. We got home at three a.m.

I lay in bed, rigid as a plank, thinking
how one day this event will leave just a spot
like a grain of rice on his skin, shrinking
in our memory to a worried ride across town.

What opera did we see that night? We won't recall
if it ended with Senta jumping into the sea,
or Tosca leaping to her death from the wall,
or Don Giovanni dragged down into hell.

This wound we watched bleed,
this shiner that yellows and swells,
will be no more real than those deeds
of legend once the final notes are sung.

Pinned

The red dog has pinned
the black dog
with teeth bared and rends
the winter air with growls
that assault our ears.

The black dog takes it,
front paws flat,
head bowed, making himself
smaller, compliant.
His ears, his neck

are nipped
as the red dog's snout
darts and swings
to clamp and release
pinches of skin and fur.

The red dog's owner
says *enough*, pries him off,
and the black dog scrambles up
and joins the others in a chase.
We humans step closer now,

scan from face to face.
I ask the black dog's owner
if he was worried.
He says, no,
now that his dog is close

to full grown, it happens
all the time, this negative attention.
Other males see him
as a threat, want to put him
in his place. His voice

is deep as granite
and he has long limbs
and a neat beard that curves
like shoreline on his brown skin.
He was a teenager

not long ago. He's so matter-of-fact,
yet the same thought must flash
through our minds, so I catch his eye
and our meaning hangs there
like breath in cold air between us.

The Camperdown Elm, Prospect Park

Props are needed and tree-food. It is still leafing;
still there. Mortal *though.* We must save it. *It is*
our crowning curio.
                                            —Marianne Moore

It's not much to look at this March day,
leaning on its crutch
as gnarled branches
slither above the dirt,
writhe toward the sky.

A museum piece, this grafted plant
withstood Dutch elm disease
and was once patched with concrete—
a crazy measure in a country
thinking only of how to build.

The fenced-in tree is bare and ugly
and could be taken for dead.
Cats climb inside,
curl their bodies in the gape
where a limb was ripped.

When I return, the elm is fringed
with nascent leaves that tip the twigs.

The sap has traveled silently
through this dancing company

who pose, these boughs
that showboat for me.

By July, its shaggy branches lift
their burden of green, rise

from the heap of roots,
lush and fully leafed.

Barn Owl

I'd swear it's an alien:
concave face,

humanoid eyes,
unearthly white glow

of feathers
too smooth to be feathers.

Dizzying spots fleck
this tentative wing

it lifts like an arm,
in greeting or in warning

I do not know.
Bizarre bird

perched in towering pine
as dusk leaches last light,

disturbing, dappled thing,
rod-stiff, silent,

whose eyes probe the darkening
where I stand in disbelief,

what do you want from me?

V.

TFW

That feeling when your senses are over-
loaded, words abuzz in your ears, your eyes
just spinning in their sockets, you're sober
as a judge but your synapses are fried
for your attention has shrunk to one screen
full of exclamation points and flashing lights
with lives polished to a glamorous sheen
and bursts of outrage spurring fight-or-flight—

until you look up, catch through the glass
a blue jay hopping in the cat's bowl
and your eyes strain to adjust as it waves
its wings, and drops of water spray, and at last
your eye muscles loosen, relaxing their hold
and there's that feeling maybe you've been saved.

Where Are the Snows of Yesteryear?

The big ones, I mean,
like that night people skied
straight down Broadway
and even the garbage bags were beautiful
glaciated ranges.

I know you remember it too:
the excitement of accumulation.
We watched from the Indian restaurant
and I pressed my hand to the window,
felt the shock of the cold.

Skiers gone, the motion of the snow
was the only motion,
snow reeling high in the streetlights,
always falling, falling
onto what had come before.

Across the room, in the very back
of the clay oven, flames played.
When the waiter brought a plate of poori
puffed with air, we tore it open,
flicked our fingers in its heat.

The Three-Legged Dog at the Dog Park

I only notice when its back end bobs
a bit off-kilter. Its tail curves upward
like a question mark, and I see the knob
where the limb's been sawed off clean. The tan fur
is smooth, covering the hip that is now
all it's got for a leg. The amputee
sits to get a treat, and I wonder how
this happened, what accident or disease
struck in its fearful past. Several dogs race
along and the tan dog seamlessly slips
into the pack, matching their frenzied pace
as they run to the bushes, yap and nip,
its three legs blended in one joyful blur
of the motion it's mastered, undeterred.

To the Figure Skater Who Fell

I saw you airborne, spinning,
arms clenched
like a corpse,

rotating like some wondrous
wind-up toy, a glinting
cylinder

of muscle and joints and bones
making air their own—not
an angel,

because angels don't work for it
and you were all effort, face
contorted

with the strain to launch,
achieving the perfect
equation

to sustain your torque. I can't
imagine how that
split second

must have felt to you—blade angled
the tiniest bit askew,
your body

toppling in random configurations,
like groceries tumbling from
a torn bag,

scattering onto the street. Later, the camera
showed your face in slo-mo, wrung
like a rag,

your mouth stretched, eyes turned skyward.
But still you stood
up again,

propelled yourself across the ice. Did you break
loose from time, wipe
memory

clean, like a fish that forgets
each second circling
in the bowl?

But you're more bird, aren't you—engineering
the immaterial
as you fly.

Why I'm Making Scones

A crack, and the shell splits,
yolk wobbles on a mound of flour.

Like the snow filling the courtyard in our dorm,
cushioning my friend's fall when he jumped.

I stir a river of milk,
and everything mixes

into sticky paste. The raspberries
sink, smear their red flesh.

His head did not burst open.
All that broke was his leg.

I struggle to separate the wedges
as the dough clings to the knife.

I set a timer in our communal kitchen
and wait for the scones to rise.

When the oven lets out its hot breath,
they're transformed. Gingerly I pry them loose,

place them in a plastic tub,
bundle up and head into the cold.

The snow feels permanent now, like trees
or buildings. Along the street it lumps

the landscape, solid as rocks. In front yards
it rises into ridges, untouched.

The sidewalk by the hospital
has iced over. I detour into a drift,

leave behind the shape of my leg.
I picture Nick, elbows on the table,

laughing, clanking his coffee cup
on the saucer, sitting up with a jerk.

Should his electric energy
have tipped us off? Did we have

any inkling something wasn't right—
that scraping edge to his voice?

When I enter, the doors open
as if by magic.

Have the scones already absorbed
the cold? My offering

seems silly now. Someone at the desk
directs me and the elevator takes me up.

The door is open, but I hesitate.
I'm afraid to face him

and what he did. He sees me and smiles,
like he's calling me over

in the dining hall. "You came.
It's cold out."

I step to the bed like this is all normal.
"It's okay. I love the snow."

Ghazal for God

I still talk to you with no reply, God,
my mind filled with King James's words for the most high God,

images of a best friend in dusty sandals and hippie beard,
and intimations of the Logos, world-spirit-in-the-sky God.

I do love nature, even caws of crows and weeds in sidewalk cracks.
The pantheists said all the wonders of creation imply God.

I want my soul to soar like something pure.
I cannot ask you to batter my heart, wring it dry. God

knows I don't want defeat. We're made for the quest
for fire and forbidden fruit—though I'm still afraid to die, God.

Don't you know, Kate, you're light and dark at once? I hush,
and hear a voice beyond the babble, a message from my God.

The Book of the Dead

Weigh my heart on judgment day. Is it light
as a feather? Or might
it speak all my sins?
That's where the trouble begins,
when the heart admits anger and spite

though surely it is good and right
to do so. Is my soul ready for spaceflight?
Don't put new wine in old wineskins.
Weigh my heart on judgment day.

Who says miracles are in short supply? Ignite
the glowing map of the brain, recite
a spell above the din
of experts counting angels on a pin.
Let's emerge into the light.

Weigh my heart on judgment day.

Scene with Dog

The dog lies twisted, head
cocked at an impossible angle,
one paw draped across her chest,
pink belly exposed

like an offering, feet splayed.
One foot begins
to twitch as I stare
at a sleep so much like death

it frightens me,
though I know she's alive on her bed,
not thrown onto the road.
Air inflates the space

under her arching ribs.
A sheath of black fur covers
all her mysterious parts
as they cycle through

their sustaining routine,
along with the heart
I've felt thrum
in moments of calm

when she's pressed against my leg,
one paw dangling
over my knee. But now
we're apart, and her neck is stretched,

head hanging in total abandon
while the belly taut as a drum
rises and falls and the muscles
under her fur ripple

as some dream roams through her lobes.
And here I am holding my breath
as this instant I'm aware
how skin and bone hold us together, both.

Thin Times

are when, folk wisdom has it, the boundary
between worlds grows loose as a spider's web
stretched in dew. Chimes tremble, yet no wind blows.
A wound heals with the full moon. But my head

says this isn't the way things work: our globe
has been plotted and plumbed and analyzed.
So why does a shimmer of something known,
as if passed down in the blood, rise

in me at the thought of this sheer curtain?
Did I slide my hand through it some night, see
a figure glowing in a dark-glossed lake?
O supersymmetry! There's a mystery

behind our motion, behind our simplest math.
There were four in the room, now there are five.
There were five in the room, now there are four.
No unified theory for being alive

exists. So stay with me a while, we'll find
meaning where we may. We'll watch dusk descend,
see the sunlight advance along the fence.
Let's dwell in doubt in this world without end.

Waiting for the Subway

Yes, there's an app for that—which train is coming when—
but look down the tunnel where a hint of gray in the distance
expands toward you. Wait and see if it's wishful thinking.
Now it seems the tunnel wall grows wider and one track

glints bronze in the shadows but you still
can't be sure. The wall curves upward, arching
like an ancient cave as you peer in, with patches
and ridges of old concrete. Things are not dark but dim,

a theater before the movie starts, and yes, it's happening:
a spot glows right in the center with spiky bursts
like a child's crayoned sun. Hold that moment in your mind,
the beam you called forth as if by force of your will,

before it divides into two focused eyes staring you down
and the subway proves the rules of perspective
once more, rumbling up to the platform to fetch you
and move you forward, always forward, into the future.

ACKNOWLEDGMENTS

This book would not exist without Brian, Clara, and Julian Deimling, and I'm grateful for their love and support.

Thanks go to Jed Myers for his generous attention to my manuscript in its various stages and his wonderful ability to help me see where the language could be tightened and refined.

I'm also very appreciative of Jana-Lee Germaine's kind encouragement and her insights into how to arrange the poems within the manuscript.

I'd like to thank everyone at Cornerstone Press, especially Dr. Ross K. Tangedal and staff members Paige Biever, Eleanor Belcher, and Allison Lange.

I gratefully acknowledge the editors of the following journals where these poems first appeared, sometimes in slightly different form:

Bone Parade: "Insomnia"
Connecticut River Review: "Jamaica Bay Wildlife Refuge"
The Ekphrastic Review: "Lascaux"
Ekstasis Magazine: "Villanelle with Tulips"
Grey Sparrow Journal: "All the Linden Trees in Bloom"
I-70 Review: "After the Opera"
Kestrel: "Turning Off the Blood"
The Midwest Quarterly: "Evel Knievel in the Café"
ONLY POEMS: "Diocletian's Villanelle" (as "Diocletian
      Upon Being Asked to Return to Rome")
Passager: "Pinned"
Pine Row Poetry Journal: "Barn Owl"

Plainsongs: "Fall"
Presence: A Journal of Catholic Poetry: "Why I'm Making
	Scones," "TFW"
Relief: A Journal of Art and Faith: "Thin Times"
Re-side Zine: "Magnolia Warbler in Central Park"
Rockvale Review: "My Heart"
San Pedro River Review: "3:45 PM"
Sheila-Na-Gig: "On Buying a Piece of Water Buffalo
	Horn as a Chew Toy for my Dog"
SLANT: A Journal of Poetry: "Hiking to the Waterfall"
Southern Poetry Review: "Waiting for the Subway"
Tar River Poetry: "By the Clock," "Ghazal for God"
Twelve Mile Review: "Scene with Dog"
Valparaiso Poetry Review: "Counting the Miles"

KATE DEIMLING is a poet and translator. Her poems have appeared in *Kestrel, Passager, Presence, Sheila-Na-Gig, SLANT, Southern Poetry Review, Tar River Poetry*, and elsewhere, and she is co-editor of *Bracken* magazine. She holds a PhD in French literature from Columbia University and has translated several books from French, including a history of color charts and an eighteenth-century novel. A native New Orleanian and longtime Brooklynite, Kate enjoys seeing nature in the city and spending time with her dog.